Antoine Lavoisier

Founder of Modern Chemistry

Lynn Van Gorp, M.S.

Physical Science Readers:
Antoine Lavoisier: Founder of Modern Chemistry

Publishing Credits

Editorial Director
Dona Herweck Rice

Associate Editor
Joshua BishopRoby

Editor-in-Chief
Sharon Coan, M.S.Ed.

Creative Director
Lee Aucoin

Illustration Manager
Timothy J. Bradley

Publisher
Rachelle Cracchiolo, M.S.Ed

Science Contributor
Sally Ride Science

Science Consultants
Michael E. Kopecky,
Science Department Chair,
Chino Hills High School
Jane Weir, MPhys

Teacher Created Materials Publishing
5301 Oceanus Drive
Huntington Beach, CA 92649-1030
http://www.tcmpub.com

ISBN 978-0-7439-0582-4

Reprinted 2009

Table of Contents

Changing Science

Antoine Laurent Lavoisier

Antoine Laurent Lavoisier (ahn-TWAN loh-RAHN la-vwah-ZYAY) is considered the "Founder of Modern Chemistry." Many scientists are remembered for their research. Lavoisier is not. He is most remembered for the way he changed how scientists study science.

Lavoisier lived in France in the 1700s. People then believed in **alchemy** (AL-kuh-mee). It was an early type of science. Alchemists did not use the **scientific method**. The scientific method is a careful, step-by-step process for proving or disproving something. Alchemists, on the other hand, looked at things such as star patterns and old ideas from ancient philosophers. The alchemists thought they could make gold from other metals like lead. This wasn't true. Many people believed them, anyway.

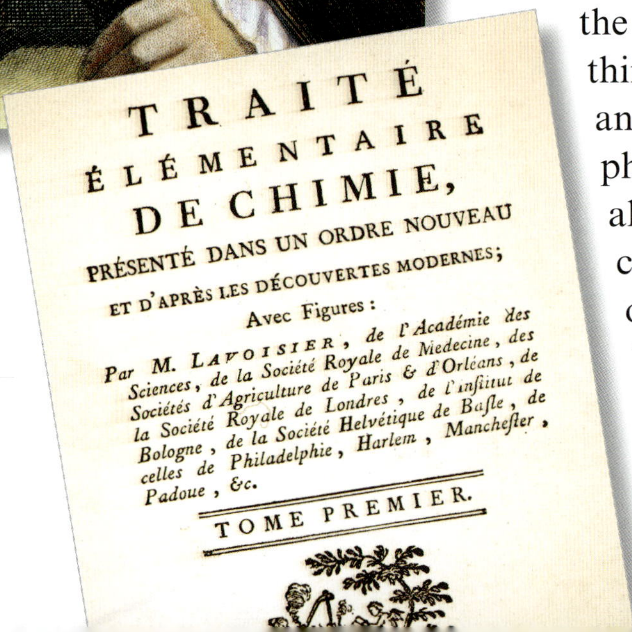

TRAITÉ
ÉLÉMENTAIRE
DE CHIMIE,
PRÉSENTÉ DANS UN ORDRE NOUVEAU
ET D'APRÈS LES DÉCOUVERTES MODERNES;
Avec Figures :
Par M. LAVOISIER, de l'Académie des Sciences, de la Société Royale de Medecine, des Sociétés d'Agriculture de Paris & d'Orléans, de la Société Royale de Londres, de l'institut de Bologne, de la Société Helvétique de Basle, de celles de Philadelphie, Harlem, Manchester, Padoue, &c.
TOME PREMIER.

The cover page of Lavoisier's book

Magic

Many alchemists were thought to be sorcerers or wizards.

Chemistry

Chemistry is the science that deals with the structure, composition, and properties of substances. All substances in the universe are made of **matter**. The building blocks of matter are **atoms**. Atoms combine to make **molecules**. When a substance is made of all the same kind of atoms, it is called an **element**. Matter, all of its parts, how it behaves, and how it is made are all part of chemistry. They are the basic things studied and researched by a chemist.

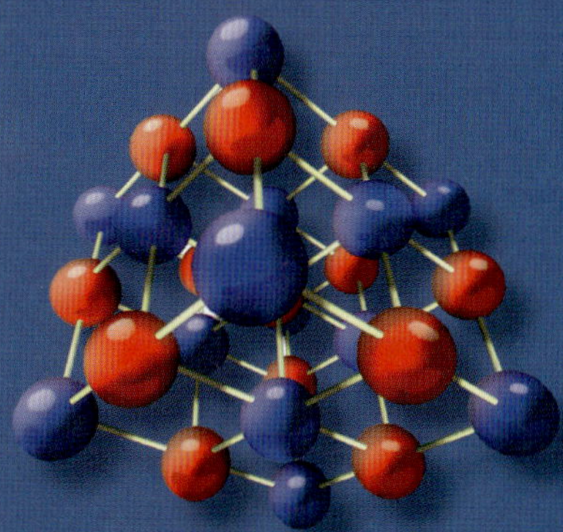

A model of a molecule

In the Beginning

Paris in the 1740s was alive with music, art, and culture. New ideas were happening in science and math. The world was an exciting place. That is, it was alive and exciting for the upper classes. Conditions for the poor were very bad.

For the poor, there were high taxes, filthy living conditions, and terrible health care. Many people who were not among the upper classes were unhappy.

Antoine Laurent Lavoisier was born in Paris, France, on August 26, 1743. His family was very wealthy. His father was a well-known lawyer. His mother was the daughter of a judge in the French Parliament. The parliament is a group of leaders who make laws for a country. The family lived a rich and happy life.

Sadly, Lavoisier's mother died when he was very young. His aunt looked after him and his sister. She dedicated her life to them.

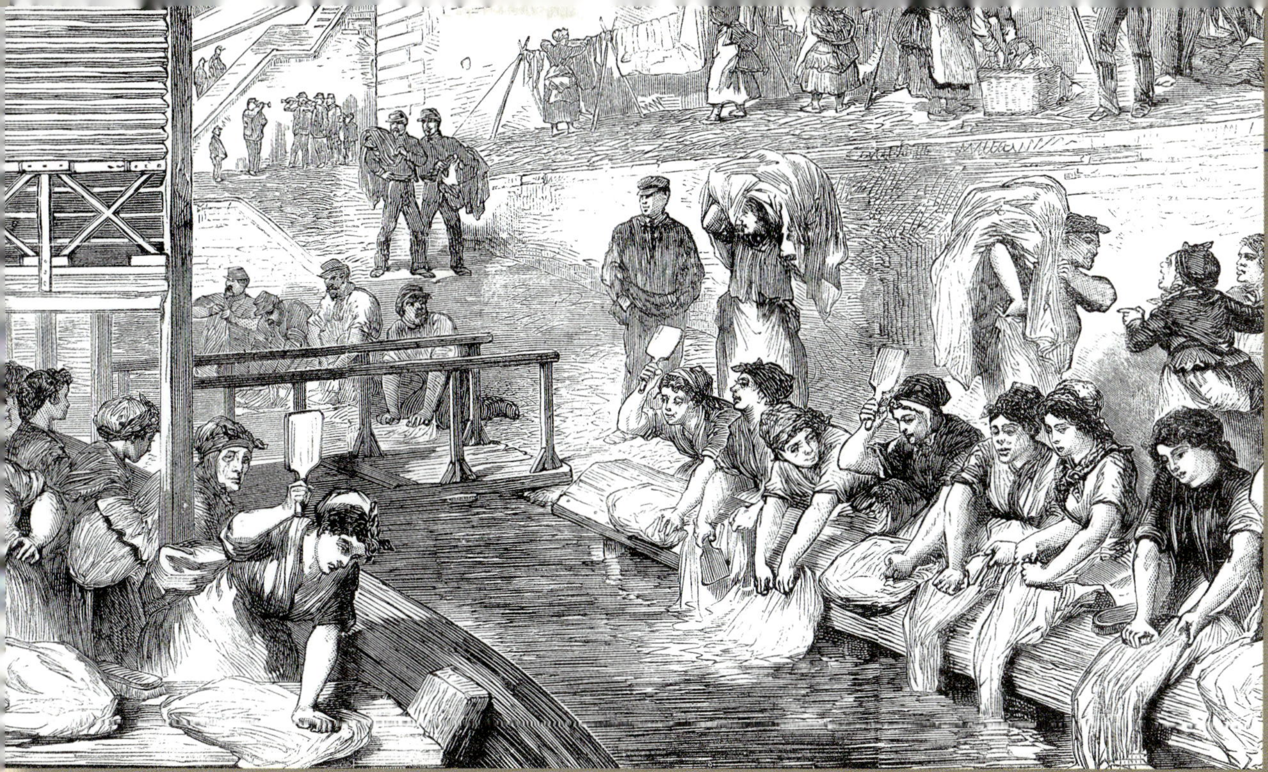

Poor French washerwomen

The Court of Versailles enjoying an outing

Lavoisier's aunt wanted him to have a good education. She did all she could to make that happen. When he was 11 years old, he was sent to one of the best schools in France. He was a hard worker. He received many awards for being a good student.

In 1764, he became a lawyer. He seemed to be following his father's footsteps. His success as a lawyer was growing. The problem was that he loved science. He loved science more than the law.

He decided to dedicate his life to science instead. First, he studied earth science, called geology (jee-OL-uh-jee). Then, he wrote and published a paper on how to improve the lighting in Paris. His early science work got him elected to the Royal Academy of Science in 1768. This was an honor for so young a person.

Lavoisier wanted to spend all of his time working as a scientist. However, he needed money to pay for his equipment and supplies. He worked as a tax collector during the day. This money made it possible for him to work at night on his research.

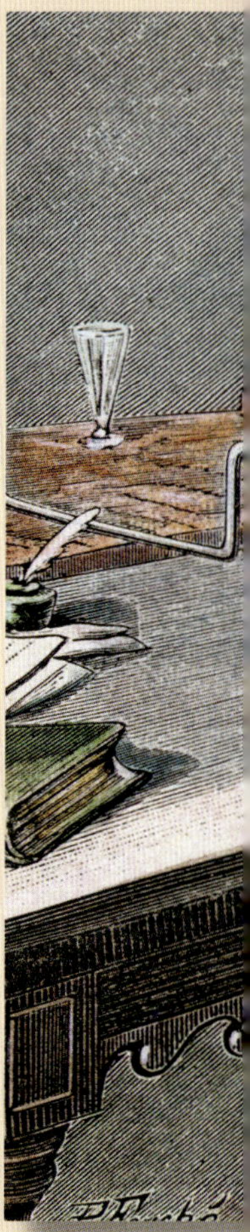

Scientific instruments of the time showing Lavoisier's oxygen experiment.

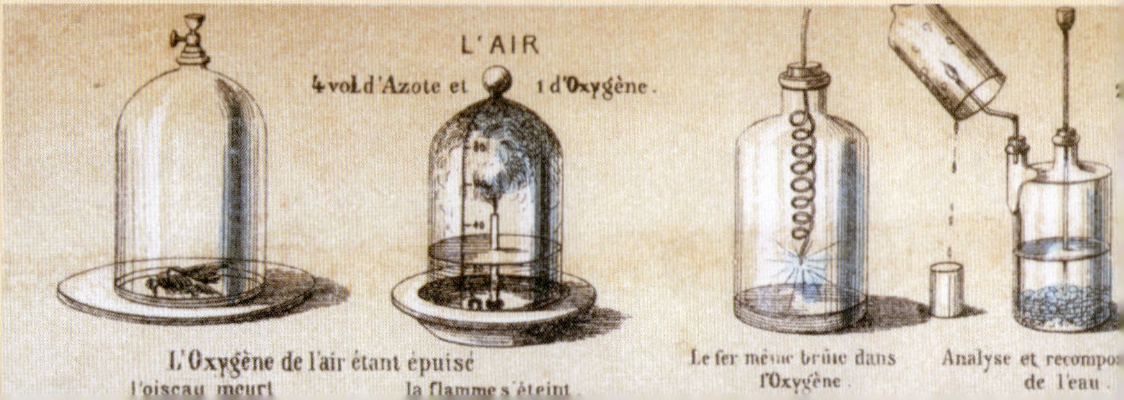

Lavoisier working on an experiment to find the elements of water

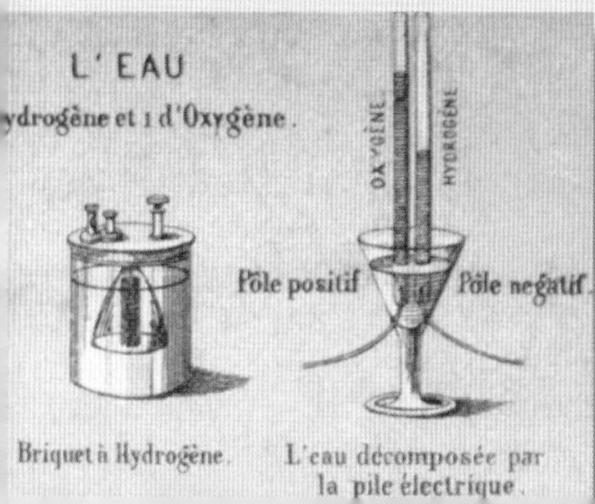

Marie Curie
(1867–1934)

Marie Curie knew the importance of education, too. She was born in Poland in 1867. She shared her love of physics with her father. He worked as a high school physics teacher. In 1891, she went to Paris. She studied at a famous French university. Two years later, she finished at the top of her class.

She became a famous chemist in the field of radiology. She and her husband received the Nobel Prize in 1903. Marie Curie was the first woman to win that award. In 1911, she received a second Nobel Prize.

Scientist and Freethinker

This is Lavoisier with his wife Marie-Anne. An air pump is shown on the table.

Lavoisier married Marie-Anne Pierrette Paulze (muh-REE-AN pee-uh-RET pawl-ZEY). She was the daughter of another member of the tax collection company where he worked. She was just 13 when they married in 1771. It was common for women to marry young then. She began to work with Lavoisier. She helped him with his experiments. She drew detailed pictures and recorded the results. She prepared them to be published. She also learned to read English, which Lavoisier could not do. This helped him to study the work of English scientists.

In 1775, Lavoisier began working for the National Gunpowder Commission. This allowed him to create an excellent lab for his experiments. His lab and his home also became important places for scientists to gather.

Pierre Curie
(1867-1906)

Pierre Curie was a chemist born in Paris. He was married to Marie Curie. The two worked together just as the Lavoisiers had before them.

The Curies studied radioactive (ray-dee-oh-AK-tiv) materials. Pierre experimented with radium (RAY-dee-uhm) on himself. He also kept a sample of it in his pocket. He had no idea that the radium was so harmful. He became frail and was in constant pain. Sadly, he was killed in a road accident in 1906. His wife continued their work on her own.

The Curies' work was so dangerous that the notebooks they used are still radioactive. Before scientists can look at them, they must sign a paper saying they know the notebooks are harmful.

Pierre and Marie Curie

Lavoisier invented this solar furnace to focus the sun's rays to heat his experiments.

Lavoisier was famous for his hard work in the lab. He was very careful with his experiments. He took accurate measurements. Lavoisier protected his findings until he was finished with each project. Once finished, he was happy to share them.

Lavoisier also studied other scientists' work. At the time, some people thought he was stealing. When he started with what other scientists learned, though, Lavoisier was able to learn new things. Reading other scientists' work became a new standard for scientists. Today it is an important part of science.

Lavoisier also shared his political views with those who came to his home and lab. Many **freethinkers** were drawn there. In France, there was a growing unease. People did not feel the same support for the government that they had in the past. Many people were very poor and unhappy. They thought the country's leaders were unfair. People who came to Lavoisier's home and lab talked about science and politics. Lavoisier believed that France needed to be reformed. He joined a committee that was organized to make a difference. The committee proposed new taxes. It suggested changes for hospitals and prisons.

Lavoisier and his friends on the committee tried to change conditions in France to make life easier. Not many things changed, though. The country was headed for revolution.

Linus Pauling
(1901–1994)

One of the most important chemists of modern times was Linus Pauling (LIE-nuhs PAW-ling). In 1954, he was awarded the Nobel Prize in chemistry. His work described the nature of the **chemical bond**. That is the force that holds atoms together in molecules. In 1962, Pauling was awarded the Nobel Peace Prize. He worked to keep dangerous nuclear tests safe underground.

Here is a fun fact about Linus Pauling. His good friend was the cartoonist Charles Schulz. Schulz is famous for his *Peanuts* comic strip. He named Charlie Brown's friend Linus after his own friend, Linus Pauling.

Important Work

During his life as a scientist, Lavoisier did some important new work. The work and how he did it changed chemistry forever.

Law of Conservation of Mass

In chemistry, a **chemical reaction** happens when one or more elements react and turn into a new substance (the product). Remember that elements are made of the same atom. They are pure. To be a reaction, the elements must act together and a chemical change must happen. For example, oxygen and iron are elements. When they come together, there is a reaction. They become rust.

Lavoisier measured the **mass** of each substance before it reacted. Mass is the amount of matter a substance has. Then, he measured the mass of new substances after the reaction. He proved that matter is never lost or gained. Even when something new is made, mass stays the same. He called this law **Conservation** (kon-ser-VAY-shuhn) **of Mass.** To be conserved is to remain the same. Matter can change its state, but its mass stays the same.

Night Owl

Lavoisier did most of his research at night. During the day, he worked at his other jobs.

Lavoisier proved that metal weighs more when it rusts. He also identified the element oxygen that combines with iron to create rust. The added oxygen makes the iron weigh more.

Dorothy Crowfoot Hodgkin (1910–1994)

In 1964, Dorothy Hodgkin won the Nobel Prize in chemistry. She used X-ray **crystallography** (kris-tuhl-OG-ruh-fee) to see the shape of certain substances. Crystallography is a branch of science that deals with how crystals are made and how they behave. A crystal is a special kind of mineral. Its molecules all line up in a regular pattern. This gives the crystal a sharply defined shape.

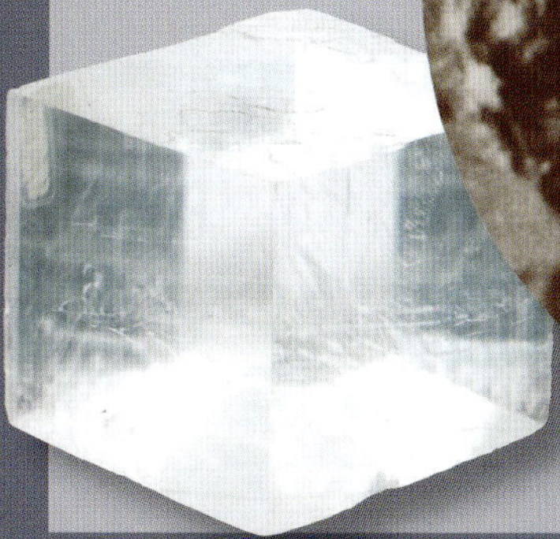

Existence of Oxygen

There are 93 different elements that occur in nature. Many elements were not known until recent times. Oxygen is one important element. It is in the air we breathe. Water is made partly of oxygen, too.

Lavoisier was the first to identify and name oxygen as an element. He named 33 other substances as elements, too! He defined an element as a substance that could not break down into a simpler substance. That definition remains today.

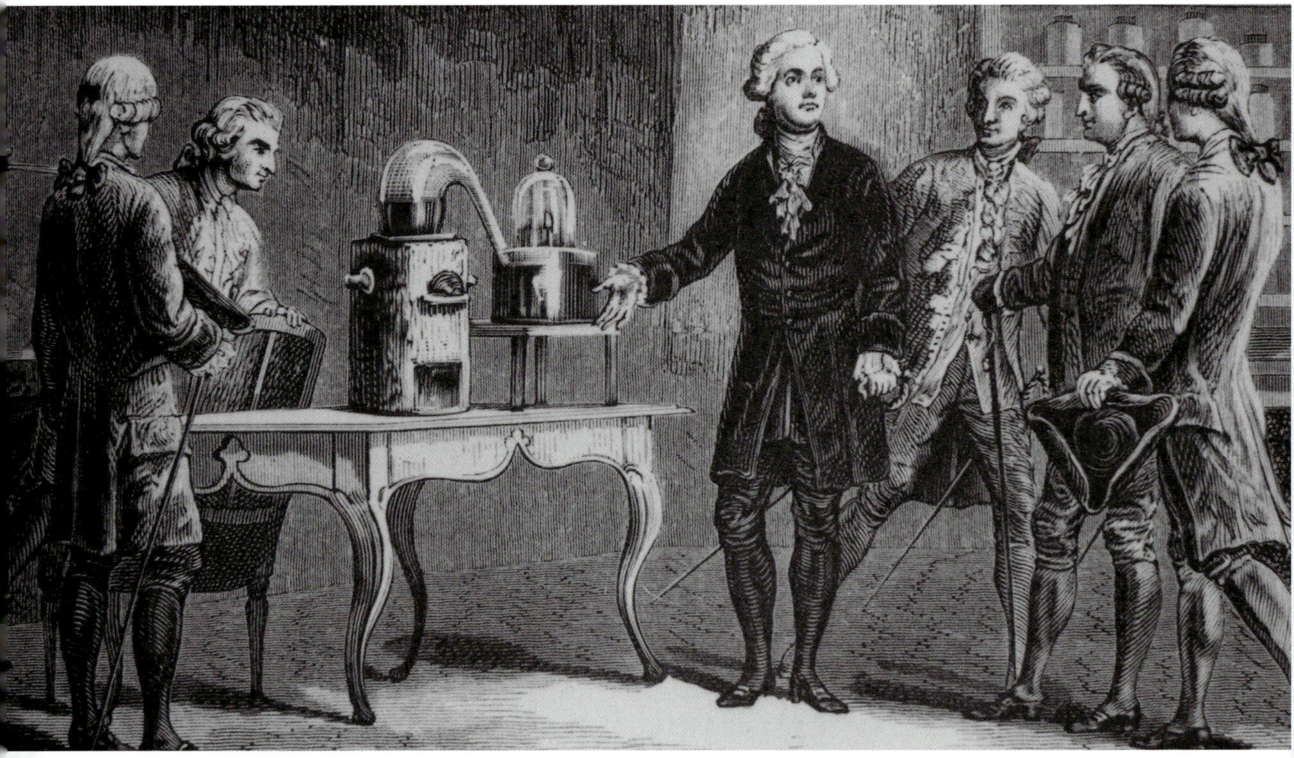

Lavoisier is shown here conducting his experiment showing that air was composed mainly of oxygen and nitrogen. He identified oxygen as a gas that burns well. He also identified nitrogen as a gas that doesn't burn well.

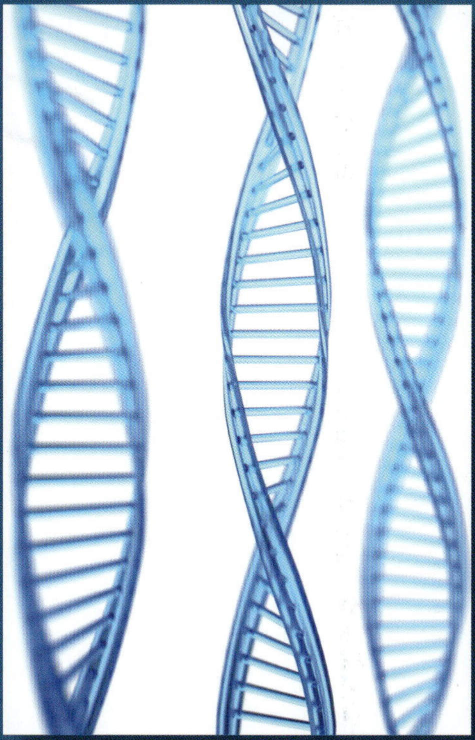

DNA strands

Rosalind Franklin
(1920–1958)

Rosalind Franklin was an important chemist of modern times. She created the first usable X-ray pictures of DNA. DNA is part of every living thing. It determines who and what a living thing will be, how it will look, and more. Your DNA is the reason for such things as why your eyes are the color they are and why you are the height you are.

To take her pictures, Franklin used **X-ray diffraction** (duh-FRAK-shuhn). X-rays can take pictures of very tiny structures. With diffraction, the X-rays bounce off the molecule and leave a pattern.

Rosalind Franklin worked hard, but her work was not well known. Many thought it was because of prejudice against her as a woman. There is some reason to believe that others may have taken her work and used it as their own after her early death.

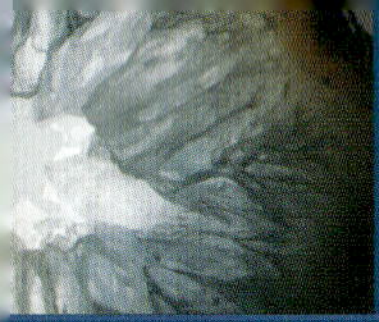

Naming Compounds

Two or more elements can combine to form a substance. That substance is called a **compound**. Lavoisier wanted everyone to label compounds the same way. Organization in science is very important. In that way, each scientist can use the work of other scientists. Lavoisier created a system in which the name of a compound was linked to the elements in it.

These are the rules for naming simple compounds with two different elements:

- The first word is the name of the first element.
- The second word tells you the second element and how many atoms there are of it in the compound.
- The second word ends in *–ide*.

For example, carbon and oxygen make a compound. It is called carbon dioxide (dahy-OK-sahyd). *Carbon* is the name of the first element. *Di* means two, or two atoms. *Ox* stands for oxygen. *Ide* is the chosen ending. Put them together and you have *carbon dioxide*.

Carbon dioxide molecules have one carbon atom and two oxygen atoms.